T0194847

GODLY KEYS TO MARITAL SUCCESS

BEST FOR MARRIED AND ENGAGED COUPLES

DAVID O. OGBEIFUN

authorHOUSE®

AuthorHouse™
1663 Liberty Drive
Bloomington, IN 47403
www.authorhouse.com
Phone: 1 (800) 839-8640

Published by AuthorHouse 10/22/2019

ISBN: 978-1-7283-3266-6 (sc)
ISBN: 978-1-7283-3264-2 (hc)
ISBN: 978-1-7283-3265-9 (e)

Library of Congress Control Number: 2019916808

Print information available on the last page.

This book is printed on acid-free paper.

Scripture quotations marked KJV are from the Holy Bible, King James Version (Authorized Version). First published in 1611. Quoted from the KJV Classic Reference Bible, Copyright © 1983 by The Zondervan Corporation.

*All scriptures are in KJV

ABOUT THE AUTHOR

DAVID O. OGBEIFUN is a cross-cultural missionary, called by God to preach the gospel of Jesus Christ to every creature and to teach them to observe all things whatsoever Christ has commanded.

He lives in Chicago, Illinois, from there, he carries out his gospel ministry to the world. He is married and blessed with three children.

ABOUT THE BOOK

Godly Keys to Marital Success is a book that emphasizes the definition of marriage. It teaches how to be successful in marital relationships and equips engaged couples with the tools necessary for a happy and lasting union.

In addition, you will discover the godly keys available to you, keys that can open doors to marital success. You will learn principles for lasting and peaceful relationships, find solutions to marital problems, collect information for raising God-fearing children, and more.

Godly Keys to Marital Success is intended for married and engaged couples, but it is a must-read for everyone.
Dedication

This book is dedicated to married and engaged couples who seek happiness, love, joy, and the peace of God in their marriage till death do them part.

CONTENTS

DEDICATION

This book is dedicated to married and engaged couples who seek happiness, love, joy, and the peace of God in their marriage till death do them part.

ACKNOWLEDGEMENT

I want to acknowledge the almighty God, my Lord and Savior, Jesus Christ, and the blessed Holy Spirit who gave me the divine revelation and ability to write this book.

FOREWORD

Godly Keys to Marital Success is a solution and a cure for marriages that face difficult challenges. It focuses on how to succeed in marital relationships. The book is written for married and engaged couples who seek to enjoy their union throughout their lives.

Godliness comes from God. Without godliness, there can be no peaceful or successful marriage. Godliness is the nature of God. Therefore, individuals must have a connection with God to become godly. To form that relationship, first we must genuinely repent of every known sin with total submission to the teachings of the word of God. When that is done, we become godly because the nature of God then dwells in us. The presence of God in your life makes you ready to make your marriage successful.

Never again spend time and resources to seek help where there is none. Your happiness and satisfaction can only be found in God and in obedience to his commandments.

Marriage is an earthly union. It comes to an end when one of the partners dies. It makes sense to enjoy your relationship and make it the best it can be because the days we live are numbered.

As you read, you will find godly keys that open doors to marital success.

I recommend this book to all married and engaged couples who desire a happy, peaceful, and lifelong relationship.

CHAPTER ONE

From the Beginning

From the beginning, marriage is defined as a union between a man and a woman. Marriage happens when a man and a woman are joined together to become one flesh. In other words, marriage is when the male and the female are joined together until death parts the couple. This was the original work of God at creation. It is undisputed.

"So God created man in his own image, in the image of God created he him; male and female created he them. And God blessed them, and God said unto them, 'Be fruitful, and multiply, and replenish the earth, and subdue it: and have dominion over the fish of the sea, and over the fowl of the air, and over every living thing that moveth upon the earth'" (Genesis 1:27–28).

The Bible is clear: all living things, both the human and

animal beings that God created, are male and female. God told the man and the woman to multiply and fill the earth after their kind. On earth, only the male and the female can come together to reproduce their kind. Today, the human race is evidence of that fact.

Marriage is between male and female when they come to be joined together and to produce children after their kind; therefore, we are counselled to adhere strictly to the work of God. Obedience to the institution that God has set will bring fulfillment, untold joy, and happiness in the union. On the other hand, walking contrary to the established work of God will incite His anger. It is a fearful thing to fall into the hands of almighty God.

"Therefore shall a man leave his father and his mother, and shall cleave unto his wife: and they shall be one flesh" (Genesis 2:24).

A married man who keeps secret or public relationships with other women is not one flesh with his wife anymore. It is the same for the married woman who engages in secret relationships with other men. The ungodly act causes fighting, quarreling, hatred, and many other types of problems in the marriage. Couples must be totally obedient to the word of God and stay away from every unrighteous act to enjoy the union of marriage.

When a man marries, he leaves his father and mother to cleave to his own wife. It is important to leave home and cleave to the new family. You cannot enjoy the fullest peace of God when you are disobedient to God's commandments. There must be leaving and cleaving to get the best out of marriage. God wants you to build your own family.

Couples who live with their parents are not able to concentrate on their relationship and build it successfully. They will be faced with various inconveniences, unhealthy distractions, or challenges from family members and in-laws that they may not overcome, and the joy of the marriage may become affected as a result.

The couple that frequently goes to their parents to seek counseling has not left their father and mother. This is also true of couples that go to their parents to report every matter. Your marriage should be independent of your parents. You are to learn to make your own family.

Instructions from God's word are the standard for building a healthy family. Deeper study of the word of God and effectual prayer are the tools to use. Your effectual, fervent prayers can help you improve the situation. Rather than going to others to speak negatively about your spouse, you can overcome your bad feelings by continually talking to God about it. He has the solution to all things. Sometimes, godly counsel from God-fearing, experienced Christians is encouraged. Decide to cleave to your partner as God has commanded. Become prayer partners. The victory is yours.

From the earlier scriptures discussed, we saw that it was God who brought the woman to the man. God should be the one to choose your life partner, not your parents, family members, or anyone else. Adam had this assurance in his heart about the woman God brought to him. When he saw her, he said, "This is now the bone of my bones and flesh of my flesh" (Genesis 2:23). You cannot have this assurance in your heart when God is not the one that brings your partner to you. There is inner peace, fulfillment, and rest in your heart when you see the woman or the man that God brings to you.

Many people go through problems in their relationships because it was not God who chose for them. They chose for themselves or were helped by other people. They chose by their eyes—looking at the outward appearance for beauty, education, position, material possessions, or other earthly qualifications. Some choose by compassion, wanting to show mercy on the woman or the man that God did not approve for them. Others choose a spouse by peoples' recommendations, those who eventually influence the relationship. It is best for God to lead you to your life partner, for God looks at the inward appearance. There is assurance with the peace of God in your heart when you are led by God. Pray earnestly to find his will.

There should be parental consent for a marriage. Marriage affects the two families. The male's family and the female's family come together in agreement to give their sons and daughters in marriage. From the beginning, it was God who gave the woman to the man, and they became husband and wife, and he blessed them.

Many difficulties in a relationship could be the result of not having family consent. Some people seek a spouse from anywhere to live with and bare children without legal permission from the required authorities. They do not have the approval or the pronouncement of blessings that are required to move the marriage forward. Also, neglect of parents or family is not in compliance with the word of God: "The woman was handed to the man, and they were blessed." Who handed you to your spouse in marriage?

The solution lies with God if you make mistakes in your relationships. There is time to walk with God and make it right. Decide to become a true child of God. Study the word of God daily and apply his teachings. He will transform your relationship in a moment: "And the times of this ignorance God winked at; but now commandeth all men everywhere to repent" (Acts 17:30).

If you have taken to yourself another man's wife or another woman's husband, God wants you to repent and make restitution. Also, if you have taken another person's fiancée, you must repent and make restitution. You cannot have the peace of God in your heart when you take for yourself a man or woman who is not legally yours. Rather than going deeper into sin, repent and make the necessary restitution so that God can show you mercy. Read the account of the man Abimelech who lived in the days of old. He repented for taking another man's wife and made appropriate restitution. God showed mercy unto him (Genesis 20:1–18).

As you read on, you will discover divine keys to lasting relationships. God will perfect all that concerns you.

CHAPTER TWO

Call to Duty

"And the LORD God took the man, and put him into the garden of Eden to dress it and to keep it . . . And Adam gave names to all cattle, and to the fowl of the air, and to every beast of the field; but for Adam there was not found an help meet for him . . . And Adam said, 'This is now bone of my bones, and flesh of my flesh: she shall be called Woman, because she was taken out of Man'" (Genesis 2:15, 20, 23).

Marriage is a call to duty. It is a call to a lifetime responsibility, one in which you become responsible to your spouse and for the children that God gives you. From the Bible verses we see that Adam had duties given to him in the Garden of Eden. He dressed the garden, gave names to everything that God created, and brought to him to see what he would call them. He named the woman that God gave him and took care of her until death.

Like Adam, you become responsible for your nuclear family. You watch over them and keep them from danger. You provide for their needs. Food, housing, clothing, and other material needs are your responsibility to provide. Marriage is not for the lazy. It is a relationship in which you are actively committed to taking care of your spouse and children.

God worked hard in six days to create the heavens and the earth and all that is in them. Adam worked hard to dress and to keep the garden of God and all that was in it. Man and woman were not made to be idle but to work and make provisions for their family. God created the woman to be a helpmate for the man. They were both created to work to fulfill their destinies. The woman is not to sit back and leave her family responsibilities to the man alone. She was made a helper to the man in all things. Working hard to provide for the needs of your family is how to succeed in marriage.

"But if any provide not for his own, and especially for those of his own house, he hath denied the faith, and is worse than an infidel" (1 Timothy 5:8). Your duty to your spouse is not transferable to others. Some people try to shift their own responsibilities to others. Dear couple, take counsel. It is your absolute duty to look after your own family. Rise to your responsibility. Save your family from shame. Find legitimate work. Learn a trade. Be proud to provide for your family. God will bless your hard work: "Whatsoever thy hand findeth to do, do it with thy might; for there is no work, nor device, nor knowledge, nor wisdom, in the grave, whither thou goest" (Ecclesiastes 9:10).

Relationships can fall apart when there is poverty in the family because of failure to work. Many people lose respect and honor for their spouse because of neglect. Some go into fornication or adultery with outsiders who help to meet the needs of the family.

Going to the public regularly to beg for help to meet your family's needs can pose a danger to your union. You humiliate your family before the public when your spouse or your children go out to beg for food, clothing, or for other material goods. It is better to rise from idleness and fulfill your God-given duties to your own household.

"Let him that stole steal no more: but rather let him

labour, working with his hands the thing which is good, that he may have to give to him that needeth" (Ephesians 4:28). The word of God tells us to do the things that are good and legitimate. Stealing, killing, embezzlement, extortion, lying, forgery, illegal business deals, and such are against the will of God. That is not how to provide for your family. God does not bless the family when you engage in such unrighteous activities. Such acts push the family backward. You are counselled to do the things that are good.

"For even when we were with you, this we commanded you, that if any would not work, neither should he eat" (2 Thessalonians 3:10).

There are people among religious organizations and other circular place in leadership positions not working to give adequate service to people under them. They depend totally on the income of the hard-working members of their congregation to carter to their needs. It is good to work to fulfil your duties to your followers. There must be work done to earn income.

Your marriage shall be blessed abundantly when you get to work: "The LORD shall open unto thee his good treasure, the heaven to give the rain unto thy land in his season, and to bless all the work of thine hand: and thou shalt lend unto many nations, and thou shalt not borrow" (Deuteronomy 28:12).

CHAPTER THREE

Godly Project

Marriage is a godly project. It is godly because God instituted it from the beginning. However, when there is disobedience to the commandments of God in the union, his presence departs. Then Satan comes in to take control of the home.

When a legal marriage is entered into, the contract becomes a project for the couple. They may have to count the cost.

Marriage will succeed when you count the cost and when you are positively committed to it to please God: "For which of you, intending to build a tower, sitteth not down first, and counteth the cost, whether he have sufficient to finish it?" (Luke 14:28).

Your spouse is your lifetime project on earth. He or she

is given to you to carry out your assignment from God. The earlier you rise to your assignment, the better for the relationship.

There is no doubt Adam had challenges in carrying out the project from God given to him in the garden, but he did not abandon the work, and he did not abandon his wife.

Every marriage has its challenges. Your challenges are your projects. You must learn to handle your project in a godly manner. You are likely to meet with similar or other challenges which may bring you unhappiness if you decide to go from one marriage to another. Also, if you seek ungodly ways to end your relationship you are deciding to leave the post given to you by God. Furthermore, you cannot terminate your marriage because of the things that you were not, or were ignorant about in the life of your spouse that were revealed after entering the marriage agreement. When you choose to leave your spouse because of sickness, joblessness, barrenness, or other emerging circumstances, you did not count the cost. They are all your projects to take care of with love. Your list of complaints about your spouse is your list of assignments. Rather than quarrelling among yourselves, seek godly ways to handle your projects.

Zachariah and Elizabeth in the New Testament counted the cost in their marriage. Though they had no children, they continued with their marital relationship, serving God faithfully until their prayers were answered. Elizabeth bore John the Baptist. The man Job in the Old Testament counted the cost in his marriage. Regardless of his many challenges, he kept true to his marriage until God turned everything around for him with a double-fold blessing.

I visited a family in Benin City, Nigeria, where a woman counted the cost in her marriage. When her husband became sick and was incapable of doing things for himself and his family, she stood tall for him and became everything to him. She gives him total care. She happily will say her marriage is her project.

When you sign an agreement, your next step is to figure out all that you will need to do to get the work done. You may have to make sacrifices, conduct research, or attend lectures or seminars to be able to deliver a good final project to the owner.

In marriage, there are godly tools to be applied so you can present your marriage clean before God, without spot or wrinkle. There must first be a decision to be a follower of God with a godly heart and faith in God, trusting him to do the miraculous. It is good to engage yourself in fervent prayers, attend marriage seminars and symposiums, learn to apologize to your spouse when needed, and seek forgiveness when you do wrong. You could also find a Holy Bible with a concordance to search for references on marriage and see what God says about it. Devote time to study the word of God and to seek His counsel. Keep up with your duties to your spouse regardless of the situation. When you apply those tools, God will bring positive change to your family. Joy, happiness, and peace shall be yours.

Nothing is impossible with God. He has enough love to handle your project. God can work with you to fix your marriage, if you let him.

CHAPTER FOUR

Spiritual Development and Training

"Come unto me, all ye that labour and are heavy laden, and I will give you rest. Take my yoke upon you and learn of me; for I am meek and lowly in heart: and ye shall find rest unto your souls. For my yoke is easy, and my burden is light" (Matthew 11:28–30).

Marriage is a place for your spiritual development and training. It is a school that will humble you and teach you to possess the nature of God, something you must do if you are to succeed in it.

Marriage reveals your spiritual condition and exposes your weakness before God and before your spouse. Therefore, it is a place where you are called to learn about the character of God to enable you to overcome and to succeed.

Jesus Christ invites you to come and learn of him. He wants you to follow his teachings to live a life of success. When you come to him, you learn of his life and character, which can positively affect your relationship with your spouse. Only Jesus Christ is a perfect example to follow. When your relationship is faced with a heavy burden, you need to come under his teachings to learn of him and make your burdens light. Every solution to your marital situation is found in the teachings of Christ. He gives a free invitation to all that would come. There must be willingness to come to learn of him and address your situation.

In marriage relationships you expose your personal weaknesses to each other. Laziness, refusing to work to take care of the family or to assist in household chores, is exposed. Sinful habits—fighting, arguing, cursing, vengeance, stealing, backbiting, cheating, hatred, overeating, disobedience, selfishness, pretense, and other such habits—are brought into the open. Refusal to pray, impatience, and unforgiving behaviors are also discovered. When this happens, they cause you unhappiness and regret in the relationship. They finally separate the sinner from God eternally if there is no repentance. (See Isaiah 59:1–2.)

Marriage is the place where you make the wise decision to humble yourself and begin to learn of God so he can help you deal with every unrighteous behavior in your life and in the life of your spouse.

Some weaknesses may not be known to you until you are married, but then they are revealed in your home. You may not be able to overcome your reactions deliberately when they appear. It is only when you are a partaker of the nature of God that you can defeat those bad feelings.

Negative reactions to the ugly behavior of a spouse also reveal a lack of spiritual fruit. Your spouse may not be the only unrighteous person in the relationship. You must also examine yourself to prove that your spiritual life is led by God. When you have no fruit of the Holy Spirit of God in you to display before the unrighteous spouse, you become the bigger problem in the marriage. You must learn of God.

You cannot enter the kingdom of God without bearing Fruit of the Holy Spirit. Your spouse is your examiner who helps you produce more of the fruit of the Spirit. You must continue to learn of Christ to produce more of the fruit of the Spirit if you seek to overcome the world and inherit the kingdom of God.

No matter how unreasonable or disrespectful your spouse is, you can bring him or her under subjection to the will of God by your Christlike life. The man Job, in the Old Testament, brought his unrighteous wife under subjection by the nature of God in him when she behaved foolishly.

Dear reader, decide to belong to God. Let him teach you the way for you to follow. You shall find rest unto your soul: "But the fruit of the Spirit is love, joy, peace, longsuffering, gentleness, goodness, faith, meekness, temperance: against such there is no law" (Galatians 5:22–23).

CHAPTER FIVE

Service to God

"Then shall the King say unto them on his right hand, Come, ye blessed of my Father, inherit the kingdom prepared for you from the foundation of the world: For I was an hungered, and ye gave me meat: I was thirsty, and ye gave me drink: I was a stranger, and ye took me in: Naked, and ye clothed me: I was sick, and ye visited me: I was in prison, and ye came unto me . . . . And the King shall answer and say unto them, 'Verily I say unto you, inasmuch as ye have done it unto one of the least of these my brethren, ye have done it unto me'" (Matthew 25:34–36,40).

Marriage is a service to God. The godly service that you give to your spouse and children is service to God. It is a place where you see your spouse through the eyes of service, and you give the service wholeheartedly as you would give unto the Lord. The services that you give are mostly what they cannot give to themselves or give back to you. God gives them to you for a purpose. He gave you the strength to be there for their weakness, therefore, cover their weakness with your abilities.

The negative behavior of your spouse may make you want to ignore your service. Notwithstanding, keep up with the godly service, knowing that it is for God. Some of us do not really deserve good things from God by the sinful life that we live daily. We cheat, we lie, we live in secret sin and more, but God does not stop doing good for us. He does not stop giving us rainfall, sunshine, food, water, and breath to keep us alive, to mention but a few. Whether your spouse is good or bad, do godly service to him or her, and by this shall your marriage be saved. It is God that will reward your good works.

As much as it is within your power, render to them what they need. Your spouse is your first neighbor. Feed your spouse; clothe your spouse; give your spouse a home; be there for your spouse when he or she is sick or faced with difficulties. You do not give good things or godly service first to the people outside when your spouse lacks them inside. Some spend their time and resources to serve relatives, in-laws, and outsiders but neglect their spouse. The order must be set right. Your marriage is your service to God.

The service that you give is not rewarded by your spouse but by God. You may face difficult challenges with your partner when you demand appreciation or a payback for your service. God is the rewarder for every good work: "For if ye love them which love you, what thank have ye? for sinners also love those that love them. And if ye do good to them which do good to you, what thank have ye? for sinners also do even the same . . . Be ye therefore merciful, as your Father also is merciful" (Luke 6:32–33,36).

What did you pay to God for all that he did for you, for all he is doing for you, and for all he will yet do for you? When you deny your spouse the service of God for any reason, you are in danger of everlasting punishment: "Then shall they also answer him, saying, Lord, when saw we thee an hungered, or athirst, or a stranger, or naked, or sick, or in prison, and did not minister unto thee? Then shall he answer them, saying, 'Verily I say unto you, inasmuch as ye did it not to one of the least of these, ye did it not to me. And these shall go away into everlasting punishment: but the righteous into life eternal'" (Matthew 25:44–46).

CHAPTER SIX

Test of Obedience

"And the LORD God called unto Adam, and said unto him, Where art thou? And he said, 'I heard thy voice in the garden, and I was afraid, because I was naked; and I hid myself.' And he said, 'Who told thee that thou wast naked? Hast thou eaten of the tree, whereof I commanded thee that thou shouldest not eat?' And the man said, 'The woman whom thou gavest to be with me, she gave me of the tree, and I did eat'" (Genesis 3:9–12).

Adam was obedient to the instructions of God for him in the garden before his wife came. He obeyed the word of God to dress and to keep the garden of God. He gave names to all that God created and brought to him, but his obedience was not yet proved.

Your relationship with God is not confirmed until it is

tested. God expects you to prove your love and service to him, like Abraham did when God told him to sacrifice his son Isaac (see Genesis 22:1–18) and like Job did when Satan tried him by taking away all that he possessed, including his wife who told him to curse God and die (see Job 1:1–22; 2 : 9). Jesus Christ also was led by the Spirit into the wilderness to be tempted of the devil (Matthew 4:1–11). Those were proved but fell not.

Marriage is a proof of your love for God in all things. Before marriage, people are seen to be zealous in the work of God; they appear to be totally committed to the activities of God. Like Adam, they are prompt in carrying out the duties of God anywhere and at any time they are called upon, but when they marry, the test of their faith comes. Many of them fall because their obedience to God shifts to their spouse. They obey the instructions of their spouse rather than God's instructions and are not fervent or trustworthy in the things of God anymore. Adam fell when his obedience was tried.

There are workers in the house of God who are not in the service of God anymore. They are in the service of their spouse. The spouse rules their life and rules their ministry.

Though they appear physically to be alive, spiritually they have fallen. God has left them.

There are preachers who glory in fancy titles and thousands of followers, but their spouse influences them against the commandments of God and against their responsibility to their followers. Some appear to be physically successful in the ministry before the eyes of the world, but they are poor, wretched, and miserable in the sight of God. (See Revelations 3:15–17.)

Many consult their spouse first in decisions about the work of God. They obey their spouse's decisions on who should be hired or fired in the garden of God. Some even get approval from their spouse on messages to be preached to the congregation at the altar of God.

The divine presence of God leaves when you shift your worship to another: "No man can serve two masters: for either he will hate the one and love the other; or else he will hold to the one and despise the other. Ye cannot serve God and mammon" (Matthew 6:24).

"Because thou sayest, I am rich, and increased with goods, and have need of nothing; and knowest not that thou art wretched, and miserable, and poor, and blind, and naked: As many as I love, I rebuke and chasten: be zealous therefore, and repent" (Revelation 3:17,19).

When you marry, irrespective of your position in life, uncountable trials and temptations arise to take your obedience away from God. Therefore, you must be vigilant and constantly stand firm in the commandments of God and do all things without wavering. Your spouse must be put under subjection to the commandment of God upon your life and calling. You must say no to anything that is contrary to the instructions of God. There must be total obedience to God on the assignments he has committed to your hands, and you must remain faithful to the end.

"He that is unjust, let him be unjust still: and he which is filthy, let him be filthy still: and he that is righteous, let him be righteous still: and he that is holy, let him be holy still. And, behold, I come quickly; and my reward is with me, to give every man according as his work shall be. I am Alpha and Omega, the beginning and the end, the first and the last. Blessed are they that do his commandments, that they may have right to the tree of life and may enter in through the gates into the city" (Revelation 22:11–14).

CHAPTER SEVEN

Commandment to Obey

"A new commandment I give unto you, that ye love one another; as I have loved you, that ye also love one another. By this shall all men know that ye are my disciples, if ye have love one to another" (John 13:34–35).

This is a commandment given by our Lord Jesus Christ to love one another. It is a commandment for every true follower of the Lord. Like every other commandment, so the commandment of love is to be obeyed.

Love must exist in your marriage relationship for it to succeed. The couple must have love one to another: "For whosoever shall keep the whole law, and yet offend in one point, he is guilty of all" (James 2:10).

When you keep all the commandments of God but offend in love you become a transgressor of the law. When you do not love one another as Jesus Christ has loved you, you have transgressed the commandment. Your marriage must reflect true love. You are commanded to love your spouse as Christ loved you. Your marriage is sure to succeed when you are obedient to this and every other commandment in the word of God. Couples who fail to love their spouse become transgressors of the commandment.

Love is giving. When you have love, you will not withhold anything good from anyone. Likewise, you do not have love when you withhold good things from others: "For God so loved the world that he gave his only begotten Son, that whosoever believeth in him should not perish, but have everlasting life" (John 3:16). Here is a demonstration of the love of God to all mankind. He gave his best to save mankind from eternal damnation. The true love of God is revealed when you give your best for the success of your spouse without looking for rewards. Your marriage will be beautiful when you do something spectacular for the improvement of your spouse without demanding appreciation. All marriages may face challenges when you withhold love or when you seek appreciation for every little thing that you do for your spouse. We do not have anything to give back to God for all that he did for us, but he keeps loving us and keeps making intercession for us.

Hatred, fighting, separation, and such will not be found in your marriage if you obey the commandment of God to love. How can you say to your husband or to your wife, "I love you," and then you fight and throw each other out of the house in front of the children? "If a man says, I love God, and hateth his brother, he is a liar: for he that loveth not his brother whom he hath seen, how can he love God whom he hath not seen? And this commandment have we from him, that he who loveth God love his brother also" (1 John 4:20–21). There must be a practical demonstration of love among you. By this shall all men know that you are a follower of God.

Love is patient. Love will always make you patient with your spouse, just like God is patient with you for the wrong things that you sometimes do in his sight. God wants you to have patience. When you are patient at the bus stop or train terminal and do not push other people down to get into the car first, you will also be patient with your wife or your husband.

When you are patient in your driving, not violating traffic rules or illegally cutting in front of other drivers, you will be patient with your spouse. When you are patient with your neighbors, not quarreling all the time, you will be patient with your families, in-laws, and with your boss at work. You do not have love when you do not have patience. Your marriage will enjoy the peace of God when you exercise patience with one another.

Love is forgiveness. Where there is love, there is forgiveness. When you feel forgiveness, you have God in you. Where there is no forgiveness in your home, it is evidence that the love of God does not exist there.

When you are a sincere follower of God, no matter how serious the offense may be, you can forgive because you are of God. Jesus even forgave the people that nailed him to the cross: "Then said Jesus, 'Father, forgive them; for they know not what they do.' And they parted his raiment and cast lots" (Luke 23:34). Likewise, Stephen forgave the people that stoned him to death: "And they stoned Stephen, calling upon God, and saying, Lord Jesus, receive my spirit. And he kneeled down, and cried with a loud voice, 'Lord, lay not this sin to their charge.' And when he had said this, he fell asleep" (Acts 7:59–60).

If Jesus and Stephen could forgive the enemies who killed them, you can forgive your spouse of any wrongdoing. Truly, the wrongs that people do to us are nothing compared to the severity of evil or sins that we commit daily in the sight of God, yet he forgives us any time we call upon him. We are not perfect in all that we do. We do wrong to people, then ask for their forgiveness. Likewise, you should forgive others: "And when ye stand praying, forgive, if ye have aught against any: that your Father also which is in heaven may forgive you your trespasses. But if ye do not forgive, neither will your Father which is in heaven forgive your trespasses" (Mark 11:25-26). Do not lose the kingdom of God because you keep hatred, malice, grudges, and unforgiveness within your heart. You will enjoy the presence of God in your home when you have forgiveness one to another.

Love is longsuffering. You suffer long with your spouse when there is love: "The Lord is not slack concerning his promise, as some men count slackness;

but is longsuffering to us-ward, not willing that any should perish, but that all should come to repentance" (2 Peter 3:9). God suffered long, waiting for us to understand his salvation. Count the number of years that you lived on earth before you became a true child of God. It took God the same number of years waiting for your repentance. There are many that are yet to be saved, but God is suffering long, waiting for them to come to the knowledge of repentance. Do the same for your spouse until he or she understands your expectations.

Adam lived in the garden for a period of time until God brought his wife to him. The man was created before the woman. Therefore, the man is older with more experience than the woman. A rib was taken out of the ribs of the man to form the woman. The woman is a weaker vessel: "Likewise, ye husbands, dwell with them according to knowledge, giving honor unto the wife, as unto the weaker vessel, and as being heirs together of the grace of life; that your prayers be not hindered" (1 Peter 3:7).

You should serve the Lord faithfully and prayerfully suffer long until your spouse understands you. There is no longsuffering when you hold onto regrets, arguments, sadness, depression, or separation when your spouse is slow, not measuring up to expectations. Your permanent love and longsuffering for each other brings your fulfillment closer. Love "beareth all things, believeth all things, hopeth all things, endureth all things" (1 Corinthians 13:7).

CHAPTER EIGHT

Child Rearing

Every child born to this world begins life with their parents. Marriage is the place where you train up your children until they become adults. The godly training that you give them from an early age lives with them forever.

"Train up a child in the way he should go: and when he is old, he will not depart from it" (Proverbs 22:6).

Child training is an everyday duty of the parent. It is your duty to equip your child with good values. The good values you teach them is what they need for excellence when they become adults.

Child rearing should be of importance to every parent. A parent must spend quality time to keep up with the growth and activities of his or her children. The good behavior of your children as they grow is your joy and reward.

The evil practices that litter our societies are the result of our neglecting to train up our children in the right way. A good parent lives by setting a good example for his growing children to teach them how to live a good life. Children grow up to do what they see their parents do. The good training that we give our children today will contribute to repairing our societies tomorrow.

A parent who is a preacher of the gospel of Jesus Christ must first take heed to his growing family, to bring them up in the fear of God before feeding the church of God, else the children will grow up and may walk contrary to gospel activities: "Take heed therefore unto yourselves, and to all the flock, over the which the Holy Ghost hath made you overseers, to feed the church of God, which he hath purchased with his own blood" (Acts 20:28).

Parents who fail to give their children decent training before they became adults have failed them. When children are not taught the right way to go, they do the wrong things, bringing shame to everyone. When they are older, it is difficult to bring about a change. It takes the power of God to do something miraculous in their lives. Therefore, it is wiser to be committed to the training of our children and not wait until they become adults to try to repair them.

Children at an early age look up to their parents for everything. They totally depend on their parents for food, clothing, shelter, education, protection, and every other provision. Therefore, the parent has total control over them. The children have no choice but to bring themselves under subjection and obedience to the discipline of their parents. This is the time that a wise parent seizes to tame, to mold, and to train up the child in the right way: and when he is old, he will not depart from it. (See Proverbs 22:6.) The growing period is not a time to neglect our children or to pamper them in the wrong direction.

Our children should be trained about decent outward appearance. As they grow, they should learn to cover their nakedness properly. Scanty or transparent clothing is unacceptable for a child of God. "Unto Adam also and to his wife did the LORD God make coats of skins, and clothed them" (Genesis 3:21). This verse tells us that God clothed Adam and Eve to cover their nakedness, not with scanty or transparent materials. Your clothing should cover your bodies correctly. Many are distracted and become engaged in sin by the seductive appearances of people who reject this truth.

Children should be taught the word of God daily as they grow. They should be taught to fear God and to keep his commandments. Your children will demonstrate good behavior when you engage them in quality family devotion where you study the word of God together. A child who grows with the knowledge of the word of God is kept by it. He will not practice evil anywhere because the fear of God is in him. "Thy word have I hid in mine heart, that I might not sin against thee. Blessed art thou, O LORD: teach me thy statutes" (Psalms 119:11–12).

Children should also be engaged in godly fellowships. They should have friendships with good people. Parents should take their children to the house of God and encourage them to participate in godly activities to serve the living God. Getting them involved in godly service and fellowship with other God-fearing people makes them good children: "And let us consider one another to provoke unto love and to good works: Not forsaking the assembling of ourselves together, as the manner of some is; but exhorting one another: and so much the more, as ye see the day approaching" (Hebrews 10:24–25).

Your marriage is the place for training your children. Disco houses, nightclubs, or other ungodly places are not to be encouraged or introduced to your growing children: "Be ye not unequally yoked together with unbelievers: for what fellowship hath righteousness with unrighteousness? and what communion hath light with darkness? Wherefore come out from among them, and be ye separate, saith the Lord, and touch not the unclean thing; and I will receive you. And will be a Father unto you, and ye shall be my sons and daughters, saith the Lord Almighty" (2 Corinthians 6:14,17–18).

It is good to teach your children to pray to God at an early age. People like Daniel, the apostles, Jabez, Hezekiah, Jacob, Paul, Silas, and others overcame trials in their lifetimes when they prayed: "And he [Jesus] spake a parable unto them to this end, that men ought always to pray, and not to faint" (Luke 18:1). A child should be taught to pray to God for everything they do. A child who starts to pray at an early age will grow to become a prayer warrior and will live a life of success. No evil will be able to overcome such a person.

Children should grow to do things for themselves without depending on anyone. They should not be allowed to be lazy. They should do household chores. They should clean up, remove trash, make their beds, iron their clothes, wash their dishes, remove cobwebs, and assist in other household activities.

Our children should grow to be independent. Parents should teach their children to help them find their abilities so they will be able to work and take care of themselves and their households. When we neglect to teach them to stand on their own, they become liabilities to us and to society: "Let him that stole steal no more: but rather let him labour, working with his hands the thing which is good, that he may have to give to him that needeth" (Ephesians 4:28).

Printed in the United States
By Bookmasters